INTELLIGENT INVESTING

Know What "They" Don't Want You to Know

Presented and written by: Dino J. LoPresti
Foreword by: Eric G. Burstock, CPA, PFS

INTELLIGENT INVESTING

Know What "They" Don't Want You to Know

Presented and written by:

Dino J. LoPresti

Foreword by:

Eric G. Burstock, CPA, PFS

Intelligent Investing

Copyright© 2025 by Dino J. LoPresti

ISBN: 979-8-9859459-6-6

SPECIAL DISCLAIMER

The contents of this book are meant to be informational only. You should consult your legal, tax and financial advisor before implementing any ideas suggested herein. Dino LoPresti and LoPresti Financial Group are held harmless for any actions or inactions individuals may take or not take because of information in this book. Dino LoPresti is not acting as a fiduciary in his capacity as author of this book.

Foreword

I've been in the personal financial advice business for nearly 40 years offering tax and wealth pathways to thousands of clients. My background as a Certified Public Accountant and a Personal Financial Specialist is very extensive in nature. Over that lengthy span of time, I've witnessed critical advice given to clients that has been misleading, subpar and average at best. When planning for our future, financial competence is vital. Having confidence in an advisor is key to a prosperous financial journey.

What you'll find in this book is (sadly) what you don't normally get to hear from most potential financial advisors. I have nearly "seen it all". I've observed many horror stories resulting from bad financial advice. These well-intentioned advisors fail to give many clients the proper direction needed in the world of financial investment. Imagine following some bad advice for years only to discover you've been led down a losing path with a poorly orchestrated strategy.

This book is so different! It contains concise and accurate information you must know before you invest your hard-earned money. In its pages, you'll find wisdom designed to truly lead you financially. I believe when you examine the contents found within these covers you'll agree with me, there is value and worth, wisdom and truth from our insightful authors.

Eric G. Burstock, CPA, PFS
Certified Public Accountant
Personal Financial Specialist

Contents

Introduction

The majority of investors do not understand how their investments may be stealing their financial security from themselves and their loved ones. When it comes to their investments, all too often the investor is unaware of the latent and excessive risk, lack of liquidity, undisclosed commissions and fees lurking within their investments. This all combines to weaken their investment portfolio – instead of strengthening it. All too often your investments are better for the person who sold them to you than they are for you.

This book has been written with the intent of opening the eyes of every investor while simultaneously saving their financial security. Wall Street and the world of investing is like the Wizard of Oz, pull the curtain back and you can see what is really happening. Wall Street and many major financial institutions both large and small have one interest and one interest only, and it is not to always help the individual investor.

Investing does not have to be that way. Investing can and should be a transparent, enjoyable and productive endeavor. No secrets, no hidden agendas, no complicated double talk. Plain and simple: do the right thing. This book will help you protect your family, protect your savings and protect your investments. I will explain how investing usually takes place and most importantly, how it should take place.

Introduction

Knowledge is Power

All investors have the desire to protect the money they worked so hard to accumulate. To protect their life savings. Unfortunately many do not know where to start, what to look for or how to begin the process of ensuring their assets are protected.

Protect your life savings from what you may ask? The answer is to protect your life savings from improper investments which usually results from bad advice. This bad investment advice I am referencing ultimately causes people, just like you, to lose a considerable amount of their money. You may have already lost a lot of money due to a bad investment or more specifically from an investment you did not understand. The reason you did not understand the investment is because it was never fully explained to you. The reason it was never fully explained is because if you knew all of the negatives, the fees, the commissions, the risk of losing your money, then you never would have invested your money in that specific investment.

You may ask yourself, "where does this improper investment advice come from?" It usually originates from the commission based selling model the investment industry adopted many years ago. Unfortunately with any commission based selling model there is potential for an inherent conflict of interest.

If something is not sold, then the sales person does not get paid. In my opinion, this is not the best model to navigate some of the most important decisions you will make with respect to some or all of your life savings. How do you know if you are receiving objective advice? The truth is with the commissioned based selling model you don't know.

As I mentioned with financial advisors work primarily on commission they don't get paid unless they sell you something. The potential arises that, when an investment is explained to you, you may NOT be provided with all of the details. You may only be told part of the story with respect to the investment.

Most people think that because they go to a major brokerage firm or bank that have nice walnut desks, rows of offices, commercials & glossy brochures you think you are dealing with the best financial advisor available. Not always true. Who do you think pays for the nice offices, television commercials and all the secretaries? You do, you the investor. Bottom line: major brokerage firms and banks hire sales people. They hire people that can sell you investments and talk you into what they want to sell you. They may do this by leaving out the most important aspect of any investment: how much risk there is, how much money you can lose, and how much of your money is lost in fees and commissions.

You may be thinking, "not my guy, he or she is different". Well maybe he or she is, but how do you really know? Read on and many of your questions will be answered. How do I know? Because I was previously employed by one of the largest investment firms in the country and saw firsthand how their business model was often better for the investment firm than it was for you the investor.

All firms operate on very similar business models. It often seemed like the client received the short-end of the deal. The client normally lost money from a combination of improper investments along with commissions and fees they did not know were coming out of their account. The client took all the risk, yet the investment firm made most of the money. I know how it works inside. I know the ONLY thing that matters to them is making money off of you. That is why the highest commissioned investments are commonly recommended. If they (the investment advisors) do not generate enough fees and commissions from your money they lose their job. Inside the doors of the investment firms the mantra is "sell the client something" because the advisor must generate commissions to remain employed.

The sell, sell, sell model is the corporate hymn that keeps the doors of Wall Street open and their wallets flush. If an employee of the major investment firms and banks is not a "born" sales person then it is only a matter of time before they will be looking for a new career. To put the sales mentality in perspective, at most major brokerage firms the more you sell the bigger your office becomes and the bigger your title.

The preponderance of investment firms and banks bestow the title of "Vice President" on their star employees who bring in the most dollars to the firm. Not the most assets, but the most fees and commissions. The Vice President title is based almost entirely on production (the amount of fees generated for the company) and how much revenue the firm garnered from those fees. The title is definitely NOT based on competence, capability, integrity, knowledge or doing a good job for the client. It is based on doing a good job for the employer.

Finding a financial advisor you are comfortable with is not an easy endeavor. Everyone seems nice if you are putting money in their pocket. Most appear to be qualified so how do you know who is acting in your best interest.

This is not an easy question to answer, yet it can be answered to a degree. The fundamental question you must learn is "how are they compensated, how do they get paid?" Just follow the money trail and your questions can usually be answered.

It helps to know if they are recommending investment that pay them a commission out of your money. It also is imperative to understand if your money has a time frame commitment. Are there steep surrender charges if you want your own money back? Will you be charged a 6% surrender penalty? On a $100,000 investment this is $6,000 you are charged just to get your own money back. Is every fee disclosed?

This concentration should be on you. Protecting your assets, getting you the best possible rates of return with the least amount of risk combined with full liquidity (access to your money) combined with a pro-active methodology where your money is invested with your best interest always being served.

My objective in writing this book is to provide you with tangible information you can use to help you protect your money that you have worked so hard to accumulate. I have tried to keep the verbiage as straightforward and succinct as possible. Read, learn and utilize your new knowledge. This book includes real information that you can use to help secure your financial future.

Losing Money is NOT
Always Part of Investing

Investing and losing money do not necessarily go hand-in-hand. However, the unfortunate truth is that most people, and this probably includes you, have lost and continue to lose a considerable amount of their hard earned money due to the fact that they have had improper investments. Investments with unknown fees or investments they did not understand with respect to the true amount of risk in which they were exposed.

This book is not a sales pitch nor is it some type of voo-doo investing. It is simply about teaching you how to gain a better understanding of the financial products that are responsible for your financial security.

Once you understand your investments you can literally save yourself tens of thousands of dollars. You will be able to secure your life savings, have peace-of-mind and no longer need to worry what is around the next curve with respect to your investments. I'm confident that no one has ever told you about how to identify the risks inherent within in your investments, but I will.

The risks I am speaking about are usually not high on the list of things to share with a prospective client. Why are they not willingly shared? After all weren't we all taught about the virtues of sharing in kindergarten? The answer is fairly simple. If you were told about the risks, fees, commissions, etc. and all the methods utilized to extract money from your account then chances are you would not have purchased the investment.

There are a lot of clever words, phrases, accounting methods and investment practices that confuse investors with respect to how your money is invested. There is a wide variety of investments available. This brief book will only touch on the most common investments that are "sold" to investors most often. They primarily include: mutual funds (retail mutual funds, not institutional funds, there is a big difference), variable annuities (not fixed index annuities), REITs (real estate investment trusts), and limited partnerships.

Many times your investments turn into the proverbial bucket with the hole. Regardless of how much water you put into the bucket, the water keeps coming out. Same with your money. Regardless of how much money you put in, you can never seem to get ahead. If you do make some gains, it's not too long before a market correction comes along and you can lose all of your gains plus more. You add the clandestine fees on top of the losses and it is no wonder you can't win and get ahead. This good news is it doesn't have to be that way. You can earn good rates of return while keeping your money safe and limiting your downside risk or eliminating it completely. The sad part is that most people don't know it's happening — they don't realize they have lost their money until it's gone.

They are not told about the negatives. Nor are they informed on how much of their money is at jeopardy of loss. Before they know it, they have lost a considerable amount of money.

The purpose of this writing is to teach you how to identify those risks and ultimately save you tens or even hundreds of thousands of dollars.

The primary objective of this brief book is not to make you an expert investor and turn you into a top money manager. However, it is written with the objective to put real information into the hands of real investors who are real people. Real people who have worked very hard for the money they have. This book contains information you can easily use to help safeguard your lifesavings.

I realize how hard it is to make money and most importantly how hard it is to safely grow your money.

I am the product of your typical hard-working blue collar family. Both of my parents were first generation Americans with their families immigrating to the U.S. from Italy. My father was a mechanic for a major tire manufacturer and my mother was a stay-at-home mom. They worked hard for every penny and unfortunately they did not always get the best investment advice. I saw first-hand what happens when a hard working family ends up on the short end of the stick when it comes to investments that were not appropriate or fully understood. Unfortunately, that same scenario is even more prevalent today than it was many years ago. Hopefully, in some small way, this little book can save someone a loss of money that they worked so hard to earn.

What You See is NOT Always What You Get

Before we go further, here are a few brain teasers. How many squares do you see?

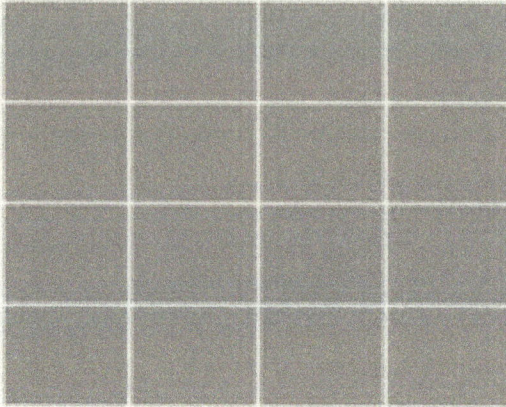

The most common answer is 16. Actually, there are 30 squares.

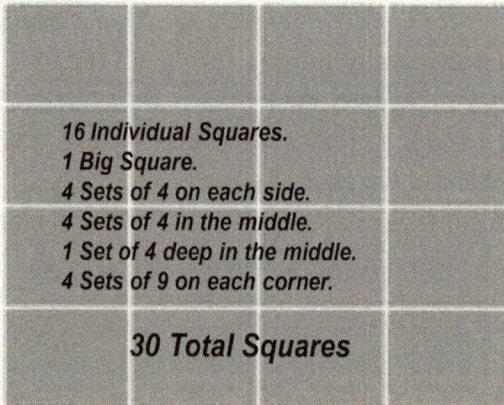

16 Individual Squares.
1 Big Square.
4 Sets of 4 on each side.
4 Sets of 4 in the middle.
1 Set of 4 deep in the middle.
4 Sets of 9 on each corner.

30 Total Squares

Here is another one:

**Which of these numbers are the most
different from the other numbers?**

1)One
2)Thirteen
3)Thirty – One

Just look at them for a second. If you look at it really close, notice the number 2) in front of the number 13. The number 2 is the odd number out. If you look at number 1) and number 3) they are both part of number one and thirty-one, but the number 2 shows up nowhere. The moral of the story is that most people overlook the number 2. They assume they are not supposed to look at the numbers before the parenthesis. They think the 1), 2), and 3) are just designating what the other numbers are. You look at these two examples and ask what do those random numbers and squares have to do with my investment portfolio? Most people don't see the hidden numbers and they don't see the squares because nobody ever told them how to look for them. Nobody ever told them there was something aside from what they were looking for.

Same is true with the investments. You think you are looking (investing) at one thing and upon further investigation you realize there is another way to look at it then you see what it really is.

Regardless of how many portfolios we review, we see the same investments and hear the same comments, . . . I was never told this . . . or they never mentioned that . . . or why didn't they tell me this . . . I didn't know that, . . . oh, so that's how it really works. I think you get the drift.

These same investment are normally recommended because they generate the most revenue for the brokerage firms and the various financial advisors who sell the investments. It is just like the Wizard of Oz, when you finally get the chance to look behind the curtain it is nothing like you were led to believe.

With respect to the same investments being recommended to almost everyone I call it the cookie cutter solution. Most all investment firms have a business model. And their business model dictates that everybody is sold essentially the same type of investment.

Cookie cutter solutions
+ People in a box
$$$ For Wall Street

Why do you think they want all investors to be in the same type of investments? The answer is simple. Corporate revenue generation. Thie goal is to keep everybody in a box that contributes to their bottom line.

Many times a person's investments can be deciphered just by knowing what investment firm handles their account. How can this be?

Investment firms have a specific business model. A model that makes the firm the most money every time a client invests. Consequently if an individual has an investment account with a specific investment firm often times that firm sells most of their clients the same investments. So there is a very good chance everyone who is a client with that firm will have essentially the same type of investments.

Just to be clear, there is nothing wrong with making money and making profits. When I have a problem is when they take advantage of the investor and when they make money at the expense of the investor and that same investor is not aware of what is really happening with their money.

It's All About the License

You may have heard the term fiduciary. According to Webster, a fiduciary is somebody in which you have placed your trust. The fiduciary has to act in your best interest at all times. So, think it through. If someone is a CEO of a major investment firm, with whom is their fiduciary responsibility aligned? Whose best interest must they serve? Do they have to look out for their clients' best interests? Or do they have to look out for their shareholders' best interest? The answer is their shareholders.

The CEO's objective is to make money for the company. If you give it some thought how does a firm make money for their shareholders? They sell investments that are commission based that generate the most fees for the company. After all, their profit comes from the commissions that come out of your pocket and the fees that come out of your investments. When you look at their model it is quite apparent they want you to invest in whatever makes them the most money — not you.

In the investment world, anyone who sells investments in the United States is required to have some type of investment license unless they want to go to jail. There's a variety of different licenses that an advisor may have. The fiduciary license or Series 65 license is the only license mandated by law that the advisor must do the right thing for the client every time. When you look at the Series 65 license it means the holder does nothing for commission paid out of your pocket

Licenses
Series 65 -FIDUCIARY
Series 6 — We are fee only, NEVER a commission.
Series 63
Series 7
"Suitability requirement" They sell you whatever they want. If you have the money They can recommend it.
100% commission based. — Anything being sold on commission has a conflict of interest.

— ever. That is the best way to be certain the client's best interests are first.

Following are some of the major differences between an advisor who follows the suitability standard compared to the Fiduciary standard.

Broker, Series 6, 63, 7	Independent Fiduciary
Paid commission for selling	Paid flat fee for advice
Non-deductible commissions	Advisory fee maybe be deductible
Paid to sell	Legally bound to provide advice with no conflicts in interest
Suitability Standard	Fiduciary Standard
Offers products recommended by their employer	Recommended investments that are in the best interest of the client
Constrained by employer	Independent
Acts as own custodian	Uses third party custodian

If Mr. and Mrs. Client meet with a commission based advisor and they have $100,000 to invest and the commissioned advisor is pushing a product that pays the advisor an up-front commission of 7%, that advisor will be paid $7,000 for selling the investment. This is a good deal for the advisor but a terrible deal for the client. The commission based advisor does not have to perform, the investment does not have to perform, the client can lose a considerable amount of money and unfortunately it does not matter to the commission based advisor because they have already been paid. It is like selling a used car. Once the car is sold and driven off the lot, it doesn't matter what happens to that used car because the car salesman has already been paid. Even if the car salesman knows that something may be wrong with that used car, they will want to sell it anyway. The only way they get paid is if they sell that car. This is the exact same model that the commissioned investment sales person follows. They do not get paid unless you buy something.

With respect to the conflict of interest referred to earlier: if a certain investment pays a commission based advisor a 7% commission and another investment that is much better for the client only pays the advisor 1% commission, what investment do you think they will try and sell you?

Do you think they will try and sell you the investment that pays them $7,000 or the one that pays them $1,000? I think you know the answer.

Fiduciary Advisor Compared to Commissioned Advisor

$100,000 Investment Amount* (*Based on 7% up-front commission and 1% annual fee.)

$7,000 Paid up-front from your money to commissioned advisor

$250 Paid quarterly to a Fiduciary Advisor.

Where do you think your best interests will be served?

If you have a current financial advisor ask them what type of license they have. If they say series 63, 6 or 7 etc., that means they follow a suitability requirement and it is commission based. Their commission is paid out of your funds in advance of the investment being made. The suitability requirement states if an investor has the money it's a suitable investment regardless if the investment is the best investment for you or not.

Unfortunately some advisory firms and advisors are now trying to play both sides. They will take the required course work to sit for the Series 65 exam. Some will pass the exam and they will be able to say they have a Series 65 and have a Fiduciary responsibility. However, they are still "selling" commission based investment. Consequently, they are not a true Fiduciary. This only causes confusion in the eyes of the client and sets a false pretense. To be certain if your advisor is a true Fiduciary, simply ask what licenses they have. If they have anything other than a Series 65, they are not acting in a true Fiduciary capacity.

Various regulatory agencies have been pushing for the Fiduciary standard to be adopted for all investment advisors. Unfortunately, some investment firms have spent millions upon millions of dollars to strongly lobby against the Fiduciary standard mandate. Why? Because they know the commission based model they currently exploit would be in serious jeopardy negatively affecting the amount of profits and revenue they are currently earning from the commission model. It is distressing that anyone would try to lobby against doing the right thing for the client.

Do you know how your advisor works? Do you know how they get paid? Is any of their compensation taken out of your money before your money is invested?

How does your advisor work? What I mean by that is: does your advisor work for you or do they work for their employer? Are they working for their employer or are they working directly in your best interest?

There's a term inside the brokerage firms, it's an acronym called YTB. It's an acronym for Yield to Broker. That's all that matters in the brokerage firms and the banks. If someone sells investments on the commission model, their number one priority is to make money for their employer.

Here is an example: if someone is a financial advisor for an investment firm and they manage say $20 million, $30 million or $50 million dollars of assets then they are mandated to generate a specific amount of fees and commissions from that chunk of money. If the advisor does not generate the required amount of fees from those assets, the investments are taken away and assigned to another advisor who will do what is needed to make the most money for the company.

They have a quota, a required amount of new assets they MUST bring into the firm to keep their job. They also have a required amount of revenue they must generate from those assets under management.

Something to Consider

What's your real rate of return net of all fees and commissions? Are the rates of return published by your mutual fund company and brokerage firm accurate? Here is something to consider.

If you have a $100,000 investment for three consecutive years and it earns 5% per year you have a cumulative return of 15% or an average of 5% annually. With compounding you would have a total of $115,762 or $15,762 in profit. Not bad.

Now take that same $100,000 over the same three year period but with a different set of returns. First year return was 5%, second year return was -15% and the third year return was 15%. Average the three years of returns together and the answer is 5%. Same return as the preceding example. Right? Wrong. Even though the average return of 5% was the same, the total monetary return was vastly different.

In the first example after three years of a consistent 5%, the total return in pure dollars was $15,762. In the second example with returns of 5%, -15% and 15% the total monetary return was a paltry $2,631.

$13,125 less money in our pocket. However, when you looked at your average return in the second example and saw 5% you just assumed it was a real 5%. Unfortunately returns are allowed to be calculated just as explained. Even though the return was the same the dollars in your pocket are vastly different. That is why it is extremely important to calculate your true returns on a monetary basis, not just as an average percentage.

Are your interests being served? And most importantly are your investments really what you think they are? The more information you have the more power you have over protecting your money.

Common Investment Traps

Trap #1 REIT's Real Estate Investment Trust

Most REIT's use investor money to build shopping centers, health care facilities and a variety of other real estate projects. They will build the real estate project, hopefully rent the space, collect lease payments, pay the associated operating expenses and pay themselves. Then they will pass through a remaining portion of the profits to you, if there are any profits left. REIT's can be made to sound like a very good investment. Many times an investor is told they can earn rates as high as 9%, 10% or more. The caveat is that there is no guarantee they will pay the investor anything. The proposed rate of return can be reduced or totally eliminated and most importantly your money is at risk.

One other major point; many REITs are non- trade-able. What does this mean to the investor? It means they cannot sell the investment even if they want. If they need the money there is no market for the REIT – it cannot be sold, thus the name "non-trade-able".

Commissioned advisors love to sell REIT's to uninformed investors because they will pay the commissioned based advisor a very large commission. That commission will come out of your money.

Let's say you invest $100,000 into a REIT (bad idea). From your $100,000 an up-front commission is paid to the commissioned advisor. If that commission is 7%, the advisor just made $7,000 from your money.

You are the one taking all of the risk, but they made all of the money. So for you to be able to just get your money back you have to earn more than 7% just to get back to where you were originally before you made the investment.

When it is a non-traded REIT, there's no market place to sell it. I had a gentleman client who is in his early seventies. His wife was diagnosed with dementia and had to go to a nursing home. He was dealing with a commissioned based advisor. Since his wife was now in a nursing home he had to start taking money out of his investment to pay the nursing home. The monthly cost of the nursing home was $6,800/month. Nearly 80% of his assets was tied up in non-trade-able REITS. He could not access his money to pay for his wife's care. He was unable to sell any of his REIT's. His commissioned based advisor "forgot" to mention the REIT's were illiquid and the gentleman would not have access to his funds. Due to the lack of liquidity, his wife was forced to apply for Medicaid, all of their available assets were spent down, and they had to borrow money just to pay their bills. Following is a quote that recently appeared on www. Reitwrecks.com regarding the purchase of REIT's:

"Indeed, it would be easier and cheaper to hire Johnny Cochran (if he were still alive) to bail you out of a murder charge than to somehow come out ahead on a non-traded REIT investment. In addition to the upfront commissions of 7% paid to your broker and a dealer/manager fee of up to 3% paid to the sponsor and up to 2.75% in asset acquisition fees, making money is nearly impossible, getting your money back is even more difficult."

Trap #2 Limited Partnerships

Many limited partnerships will invest in a variety of enterprises such as logging operation, mining, natural gas etc. If that company ever makes a profit they will pass through some of the investment return to you. Limited Partnerships, just like REIT's also have very high upfront commissions.

The limited partnership will often project a very high rate of return. It's only a projection. They can cut that rate of return any time they want. The investor plunks down a big chunk of money, the commissioned based advisor takes a big chunk of money out for their commission and you have the potential to earn very minimal returns. Many limited partnerships are also non-traded, so if you ever need your money you can't get it out.

REITs and Limited Partnerships are somewhat common however the next few investments I will reference are very common. They are mutual funds and variable annuities.

Variable annuities are so bad I can write a complete book just on the perils of variable annuities. You see them advertised on television, in the magazines, newspapers, post cards, dinner seminars and just about everywhere else. They are always pushed by the commissioned advisors. Why? Because they pay a very large up-front commission and also have very high annual fees, which by the way are not normally fully disclosed to the investor.

Trap #3 Variable Annuities

Variable annuities are one of the most misunderstood investments. The reason they are not understood is primarily due to the reason that whoever sold the product didn't bother to tell the investors everything they needed to know. The negatives of the investment are sometimes conveniently left out.

One of the worst things about variable annuities is the buried fees and the risk to your money. The fees that are rarely disclosed to the investor normally average 3-4%.

Therefore, if you have a $100,000 variable annuity, $3,000 - $4,000 is being taken from your account every year. If you have a $300,000 variable annuity, $9,000 - $12,000 is being taken out of your account every year and so on.

The problem with the fees is that most investors do not know the large amount of money is being deducted from their account. Additionally, the fees do not show up on the statement. To find the fees you need to read the prospectus which normally ranges in size from 150 pages to 250 pages in length.

I have seen prospectus' up to 400+ pages in length. How bad must an investment be if the attorneys need to write 400 pages disclosing all of the risks. Here is a general rule: the longer the prospectus the worse the investment.

To complicate matters further, the fees are usually disguised with arbitrary terms such as mortality risk expense charge, management override charge, fund expenses, gross return, rider assessment along with a host of other creatively worded verbiage to keep the uninformed investor in the dark with regards to the money that is being taken out of their account.

To put it bluntly, when a variable annuity is sold many times key information is left out of the explanation. Is this a simple oversight or an intentional omission? Information the investor desperately needs to know to make an informed decision many times is left out of the conversation.

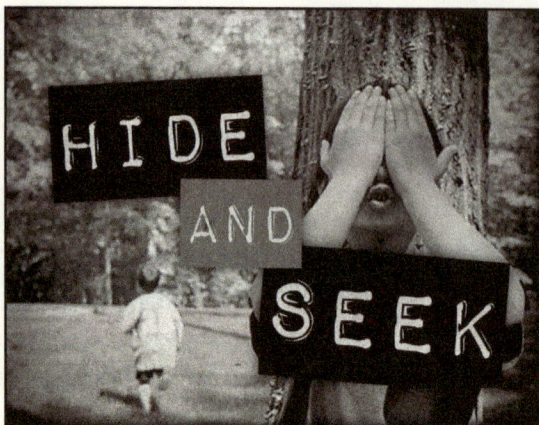

Where are all the variable annuity rates?

Conveniently found in the 200+ page
prospectus that is rarely reviewed.

M&E	1.40%
Adm	0.15%
Rider	1.55%
Fund Exp.	1.55%
	4.66%*

(*Not all variable annuities have fees of 4.66%; some are lower and
some are higher. "Please refer to prospectus for details!")

A complete explanation of variable annuities is outside the scope of this book. However, I strongly feel you need to understand the basic moving parts of a variable annuity to protect yourself from purchasing this product when it is necessary. A variable annuity is, in many cases, an "uninsured" securities/insurance product that provides investment options, much like mutual funds. The following section covers mutual funds, so for the sake of brevity and the elimination of redundancy I will leave the mutual fund explanation for the upcoming section.

Variable annuities simply cost too much. Variable annuity fees usually dwarf those charged by other investment. This is easy to understand when you realize there are two players involved instead of one. And both of those players need to be paid. The two player are the insurance company and the mutual fund company. A variable annuity is nothing more than a very complicated and expensive way to buy mutual funds. As previously mentioned, the average variable annuity passes along expenses of 3 – 4 percent per year.

The death benefit of the variable annuity is always mentioned as some sort of great positive for this questionable investment. The death benefit becomes the crutch when all other arguments fail. Here is one of the variable annuity's dirtiest sections: the variable annuity's death benefit is often pointless or superfluous. However, the "death benefit" is the aspect of the variable annuity that is often times stressed to the potential customer.

With a variable annuity, an insurer guarantees that heirs will receive at least the contributions made into the annuity. One important fact that is often left out of the conversation is the death benefit paid is equal to the original investment, less any withdrawals. Additionally since most variable annuities are ten year contracts, simple math tells us that an exorbitant amount of fees are coming out of that variable annuity. You may get your original principal back, but you do not get your fees back or any money you may have withdrawn. So you are essentially paying fees for ten years or longer to make certain your heirs get your original money back. Not the best use of your money.

The dubious death benefit of the variable annuity is costing people big money. Undoubtedly, the variable annuity company is charging 5 — 10 times the economic value of the death benefit guarantee. A study by researchers at York University in Canada and Goldman Sachs a few years ago suggested that the insurance fee that is embedded in the variable annuity is way out of proportion with what it is truly worth. A typical life insurance charge is 1.35% (although it can run as high as 1.75%) which would work out to a cost of $3,125.00 per year for a $250,000 variable annuity. Using the study's comparison, a fair and normal death benefit charge would only be $570.00 annually for a male age 50 and $398.00 for a female the same age.

If you are unfortunate enough to own a variable annuity there are ways out. Be aware that variable annuities usually have steep surrender penalties. You need to be aware of the surrender charges. There are some cases when a variable annuity has a surrender charge and it still makes sense to liquidate it. This is because the fees you are paying on an annual basis will ultimately be more than you will pay in surrender penalties. This is not always the case. Every situation is different. Just be certain you are making the best decisions for your circumstances.

Furthermore, non-qualifies variable annuities may grow on a tax deferred basis. If you simply surrender the variable annuity in a non-qualified account you open yourself up to a possible negative tax consequence. There is a mechanism in place called a 1035 exchange where you can roll over a variable annuity to a fixed index annuity to mitigate any potential negative tax consequence. A fixed indexed annuity can be structured with no fees and protection of principal. Even though it is an annuity it is totally different than a variable annuity. There are some very good annuities and some very bad annuities. The variable annuities are usually not the best. Now for the discloser: I am not providing tax advice, please consult your tax advisor. Additionally, other factors must be considered when investigating a possible 1035 exchange.

Trap # 4 Mutual Funds

Mutual fund managers have made it quite clear. They will go to endless lengths to make Americans believe that speculating in the stock market is synonymous with investing. On average only 4% of US Stock Funds have beaten the actual performance of the S&P. Financial sales people continually speak of a mythical mutual fund that will produce a 10% annual rate of return "over the long haul". This is a stark contrast to the data. Dalbar, one of the nation's largest research firms found that actively managed mutual funds have only yielded returns of 3.7% over a twenty year period. The S&P 500 Stock Index has essentially gone nowhere in the past 12 years and ultimately delaying retirement for a large percentage of the population.

Bill Gross, former CEO of PIMCO said investors should think again about the age-old "buy and hold" strategy because consistent annual returns are a thing of the past. Gross points out stocks have averaged a 5.6% annual gain on an inflation-adjusted basis since 1912. However, he labels that rate of return as a "historical freak" that isn't likely to be duplicated anytime soon due to slowing economic growth around the globe.

There are 3 different types of mutual funds normally recommended by various financial advisors. There is an A, B and a C. Look on your statements to identify your mutual fund holdings. Mutual funds are identified by a five letter symbol ending in "X". An example would be AAAAX. The difference between the three different types of mutual funds are how the investment advisor is paid.

With an "A" mutual fund, the fees are taken out up-front before you even invest into the mutual fund.

For example; lets say an investor has $25,000 to invest in an "A" mutual fund. The "A" funds will have a range regarding how much they will take out for the commission. The amount deducted will normally be in the 4% - 5.75% range. With our $25,000 example at a 5.75% up-front commission of $1437 being deducted from your account prior to investing. Let's walk it through; you have $25,000 to invest, you are presented with an "A" mutual fund. With a 6% up front commission $1437 is taken out of your account, eventually $23,562 is invested. So you need to earn more than a 6% return just to get your original investment back. Not such a great deal. Hold on, there are more fees. Many funds charge what is called a 12B1 charge which is approximately .25%. The 12B1 charge is used for marketing expenses.

All of those visual commercials and ads of the attractive retired couple on their sail boat or walking through their grape vineyard put out by various mutual funds are paid for with investors' money. More than $12 billion is deducted in 12B1 fees on an annual basis. But wait, there's more...Many mutual funds charge approximately 1.25% for what is called "annual operating expenses" and don't forget about the up-front commission paid from your money.

Total all those fees up and you are paying a whopping 7.25% in fees. And chances are pretty high you had no idea those fees were coming out of your account.

It is rare all of the fees are ever disclosed. If somebody wants to invest $100,000, do you think the commissioned advisor would say "by the way, we're going to take out $5,750 before we invest your money – is that alright with you?" Nobody will ever agree to that. They conveniently leave the fee structure out of the discussions.

Mutual
Funds
"A"
"B"
"C"   Fees

12b-1 Fees (Advertising)
$12 Billion / Year

Many mutual funds you need to earn 6% just to break even and get your money back they took out for commissions.

Next are the "B" mutual funds. With a "B" fund they assess you an average of a 6% deferred sales charge if you sell it the first year, 5% the second year and so on. "B" funds also assess the 12B1 fees and the annual operating expenses as previously described.

"C" mutual funds are next. "C" funds were conceived in an attempt to compete with so-called no load mutual funds. There's no such thing as a "no load" fund by the way. They all have a load somewhere.

But a "C" mutual fund has a reduced front load which might be 2 ½% and you think hey, that's not too bad 2 ½% compared to the "A" fund at 5 ¾% so I'm saving 3% upfront. Hold on, not so fast.

What the "C" does is they have about a 2 ½% annual management fee and they have about another 1% what they call an annual offering fee. So you are going to pay 2 ½% upfront, and then about 3 ½% every year over and over for a total of 6%.

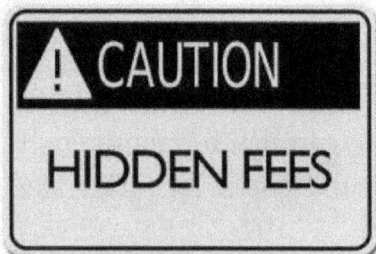

The Real Cost of Owning A Mutual Fund

Since mutual funds are commonly owned by so many investors, I felt it prudent to elaborate a little more on mutual funds with respect to their fees and expenses that most people never consider.

Few investors understand the total cost of a fund, including tax, transaction and advice fees.

In all our years of business, our firm has never had an initial meeting with an investor who completely understood the total costs of the mutual funds they owned. The following seeks to simplify the many complexities of mutual fund expenses so investors are able to discover the true costs associated with mutual fund ownership. To simplify this topic, six different costs will be evaluated: expense ratio, transaction costs (brokerage commissions, market impact cost, and spread cost), tax costs, cash drag, soft dollar cost and advisory fees.

Expense Ratio

The expense ratio is frequently the only cost that many investors believe they pay when owning a mutual fund. The expense ratio is frequently used to pay marketing costs, distribution costs and management fees. This ongoing cost can be identified by reading a mutual fund's prospectus. The average U.S. Stock fund now costs .90% per year according to a recent Morningstar article.

Transaction Costs

A study found U.S. Stock Mutual Funds average 1.44% in transaction costs per year . These costs can be difficult to determine, are not easily found in the prospectus and are not included in the aforementioned expense ratio. A group of cost conscious investors called the Bogleheads breaks down transaction costs into three categories: brokerage commissions, market impact, and spread cost.

1. **The first type of transaction cost is brokerage commissions.** Brokerage commissions result from mutual fund managers buying and selling stocks for mutual fund investors inside of the fund company's brokerage account(s). Discovering the additional expenses due to turnover can be a difficult endeavor.

   This task can be accomplished by making estimates based on information found in the Statement of Additional Information: a document mutual fund companies must make available upon request, but don't generally distribute to investors.

2. **The second transaction cost even more difficult to estimate is market impact cost.** Market impact cost is essentially "a mutual fund making a large transaction in a stock will likely move the stock price before the order is completely filled." This negatively affects mutual fund owners in three distinct ways. First, individuals receive less favorable prices on certain stocks being bought and sold. This occurs when an investor's mutual fund manager is buying or selling large quantities of stock that drives the price artificially higher or lower. Second, a fund manager

may alter its investment management strategy to avoid excessive market impact costs.

This can happen if a manager chooses to enter and exit stock positions over long time horizons in an effort to mitigate sudden short term movements in the securities it is trying to sell or acquire. Last, a mutual fund manager may be forced to include less favorable stocks in its portfolios to alleviate the market impact pressure on its favorite stocks. Market impact cost can be a lose-lose situation for mutual fund investors because they may get unfair pricing on both the buy and sell side of stock transactions in addition to having their mutual fund managers compromising their stock picking prowess to avoid excessive costs.

3. **The final transaction cost is called spread cost.** This cost also occurs when a mutual fund manager buys and sells stocks for mutual fund owners. Spread cost reflects the difference between the best quoted ask price and the best quoted bid price. This cost is also difficult to quantify. Generally, it is more excessive when a mutual fund is trading international or smaller, less liquid stocks.

Transaction costs can add substantially to the overall expense of an investor's mutual fund. In addition to being substantial, these costs are nearly impossible to accurately quantify.

Tax Costs

Many investors pay more than their fair share in taxes when owning mutual funds. This problem is most transparent when mutual funds are owned outside of an IRA, Roth IRA, 401(k), or other tax-deferred accounts. An investor who buys into a mutual fund that is holding stocks that have appreciated prior to the purchase of the fund runs the risk of paying for these stocks' capital gains taxes. Essentially, even if the investor did not benefit from the stocks' gains, this investor will share proportionately in taxes due from the sale of these appreciated stocks when the mutual fund manager makes a change. Ultimately, one can end up paying taxes on investments that other investors profited from. Before purchasing an actively managed mutual fund in a taxable account, an investor should consider contacting the company to determine the level of embedded gains within the mutual fund. According to Morningstar the average tax cost ratio for stock funds is 1% to 1.2% per year.

Cash Drag

Another cost of owning a mutual fund is cash drag. Cash is frequently held by mutual fund managers to maintain liquidity for potential transactions and potential redemptions by mutual fund owners. This may stifle the performance of a mutual fund if stocks increase in value greater than the cash held. According to an independent study, the average cost from cash drag on large cap stock mutual funds over a 10-year time horizon was .83% per year. This cost results from investors paying the mutual fund's expense ratio on 100% of the money invested despite the fact that not all of the assets are invested into stocks or other securities. Someone who holds cash in a bank savings or money market account on an individual basis generally does not have to pay these extra costs.

Essentially, buy and hold investors are subsidizing other investors' liquidity needs. It should be noted that cash held within a mutual fund could be beneficial during a time when stocks do poorly and incrementally more expensive when stocks perform well relative to cash.

Soft Dollar Cost

One of the most difficult mutual fund expenses to estimate is called soft dollar cost. This cost comes into play when mutual fund managers are buying and selling stocks within the mutual fund's brokerage account(s). Frequently, mutual fund managers may direct the money being managed to brokerage companies providing them with research and/or other services, even if the brokerage companies are not providing the most cost efficient brokerage commissions involved with buying and selling stocks.

Essentially, this is a quid pro quo arrangement. The mutual fund manager gets special services and/or research, and the brokerage company gets the brokerage business at a premium rate. This effectively keeps this cost out of the public's eye, giving a fund the artificial appearance of lower than actual expenses. A research study suggested that U.S. soft dollar brokerage commissions may total $1 billion annually, or up to 40% of all equity trading costs.

Advisory Fees

The final cost is only relevant to individuals working with investment advisors who select loaded mutual funds for their clients. Many fee-based advisors will manage an investor's portfolio for an annual fee commonly ranging from .25% to 3.50% of the portfolio's balance. This fee is required to be disclosed on investors' statements, and is charged in addition to the other mutual fund costs discussed. Hedge fund managers charge a management fee plus a percentage of earnings.

Cost Summary

The following summarizes the average quantifiable costs described. Advisor and soft dollar costs are excluded due to the large range in advisory fees and the difficulty of quantifying soft dollar costs.

When working with a financial advisor, it is important to add the commission and the advisory fee to the mutual fund costs listed below for an accurate depiction of total potential costs.

Non-Taxable Account	Taxable Account
Expense Ratio .90%	Expense Ratio .90%
Transaction Costs 1.44%	Transaction Costs 1.44%
Cash Drag .83%	Cash Drag .83%
--	Tax Cost 1.00%
Total Costs **3.17%**	Total Costs **4.17%**

As illustrated, hidden costs have infiltrated the mutual fund industry and are being paid by many unsuspecting investors.

Once someone invests in commission based investments it is the exact same way the used car salesman gets paid. You buy the product and the salesperson gets paid. It does not matter if the product performs or not, the salesman already got paid. So if the product does not perform, the sales person does not have a vested interest in your success – because they already got paid – from your money.

With the used car, you drive off the lot and the engine blows up - - - so what, the sales person has already been paid. It's the same with these types of investments. The brokerage firms, mutual fund companies and sales person does not have a vested interest in your success.

Another large negative with many mutual funds is that in a mutual fund the money truly cannot be managed. For example, when someone is invested in a traditional mutual fund and the markets begin to head south normally their fund will also lose value. Of course all investments will fluctuate. What I am referencing is over a prolonged period of time when the mutual fund value continually declines and loses 10%, 20%, 30%, and more. The mutual fund investor looks at their depleted funds and wonders why doesn't the mutual fund manager sell out? Why don't they get rid of these things and move the money to a safe cash account and wait for things to settle down?

Money cannot be managed in a mutual fund.
By prospectus, the fund must keep the majority of the money
invested at all times. Can not go to cash when the market declines.
You are told to hold, because they can NOT move your money.

**You must sit idly by and watch
your account lose money...**

Simply put they can't, they are not allowed. There are strict guidelines on how these large mutual funds can move money around. Some of these mutual funds are very large, $10 billion and up, some as large as $150 billion. With such a large amount of money the rules mandate that the mutual fund managers must have the majority of the money invested at all times.

So what that means is that when the market is going down, those fund managers cannot go to cash. If they were to go to cash it would be like a run on the bank. All of these extremely large mutual funds trying to sell their losing investments would cause the market to decline even further and faster. So they are forced to stay invested and you the investor must sit idly by and watch your account lose money.

In a declining market, if you call your advisor up and ask what is going on with respect to your account losing money, you are normally told one of two things. The most common response is , "Hold onto it, we're in for the long term", "stay in, don't worry about it, it will come back". Or they will say, "don't worry, it is just a paper loss". Baloney, it is NOT, just a paper loss, it is real money and you just lost it.

Real World Examples

The Wall Street Journal had a very good article making reference directly to my point. The title of the article was <u>Why Brokers Want You to Buy Mutual Funds and Other Questionable Investments: Just follow the money.</u> The article included the following statement: "Variable annuities and mutual funds are Wall Street's most dubious offerings. Brokers are relentless in pushing them even when they aren't in the client's best interest. Mutual funds may appear to be expensive but they are a bargain when compared to variable annuities." The reason being is the average variable annuity will pay, to whoever sold it, 6%-7% upfront commission and it will take out 3%-4% per year out of your investments which is why you can't make any money. Mutual funds work the same way. There was an article in Forbes which was called <u>Shelter Skelter</u> about a variable annuity.

The article appeared recently discussing the sales practices of variable annuities. The article states a major brokerage firm persuaded an 81 year old widow to put her entire life savings of $384,210 into two variable annuities. The advisor, not the brokerage firm, pocketed a whopping commission of 6.75% on her investment. The advisor made $25,900 on one sale. That's the whole point with the commissions. Any time you have a commission based model there's an inherent conflict of interest.

The same advisor certainly could have recommended a much better investment for the 81 year old widow that would have been a lot safer, but it goes to question – does the advisor make a $2,000 commission or do they make $26,000? All too often, greed wins and the client loses.

The article continues with the woman quoting, "I got ripped off royally..." she had to mortgage her house to meet expenses because her money was tied up and she suffered such great losses.

Another article appeared in Newsweek and it addresses variable annuities. The title of the article is "One Faulty Investment". The author Jane Bryant Quinn begins the article by writing, "You rarely find me so deeply angry at a common investment product that I dream of blowing to smithereens. Especially one that is sold by America's leading brokerage firms and financial institutions, commands nearly $400 billion in assets and sounds like a winner for retirees. But stand back I am going to light my fuse. My target? Tax deferred variable annuities. What a laugh. It will cost you more in taxes and penalties and risk your security. I cannot imagine a personal financial situation where I would ever recommend a variable annuity."

The last example regarding variable annuities was in The Wall Street Journal. The article was titled <u>Variable Annuities Dismay Investors</u>. It is about a retired couple, they had saved up $479,000 in an individual retirement account. The couple had accumulated most of it during the husbands 30 years as an employee of Chevron. He recently retired and was looking for some financial advice. Speaking to one of his friends, it was suggested that he speak with his friend's financial advisor. Well, the financial advice he received was not the best. The retired gentleman was told to invest in variable annuities. He followed the advice and watched his value go down and down.

The article states when the gentleman realized they could move their account to a different advisor they had lost all but $130,000 of their life savings. The retired individual was forced to return to the work force at age 67. His wife also had to look for employment. They were also forced to mortgage their home to meet expenses.

So the retired couple lost $348,000. You have to ask yourself, why is there so much bad investment advice out there? Seems like everywhere you turn, someone is hiding something, not doing what is in your best interest and not providing you, the investor with all of the facts. But why? The answer is relatively simple: the commission based model is alive and well.

Doesn't seem quite fair does it?

Referencing another article that appeared in the publication Best Life answers the question as to why there is so much bad investment advice freely given to unsuspecting investors. Remember when I previously mentioned all of the different investment licenses available? I mentioned the Series 65 which is the fiduciary, and the series 63, 6 and 7 which are the commissioned based licenses.

A popular magazine called Best Life had an article titled "Choosing a Financial Advisor." It references a gentleman, who we will call John, who lost more than $1,000,000 due to improper advice. The article puts into context why there is so much bad investment advice being churned out by a multitude of investment brokers.

The article states that John needed some investment advice. After decades of hard work he had managed to stash away more than two million dollars in savings. He had a goal of being financially independent for life. If someone has saved two million dollars I think it's safe to say they have done a pretty good job of saving. But just like most investors he was looking for a safe investment with better returns. So John hired a prominent national brokerage firm to oversee his investments.

The firm put his investments in a program supposedly steered by top brokers – supposedly the best of the best, the brightest of the brightest. Well how did those experts handle his life savings? When the market started its decline no one called to suggest moving John's investments into cash to protect his money. If these investment advisors were supposed to be so qualified and they worked for one of the largest investment firms, you would think they would have access to data supporting the fact that the market was overvalued and ready to take a plunge downward. The fact of the matter is, they all have that data, however they normally do not act on it. Why? Because they want to keep you fully invested at all times. The longer you are invested, the more money they make.

As the market spiraled down, no one ever called. Finally John got tired of waiting and called in a panic to inquire what was going on with his account. When he called in a panic he was told, "don't worry everything's on track, we're in this for the long term, anyway, it is only a paper loss".

Begrudgingly he listened to the advice and decided not to sell. A few more months went by and his account value continued to plummet downward. Within two years John lost all but $900,000. He lost $1.1 million dollars in a little over two years.

So the brokers were billed as the best of the best but things were going down and down and no one said anything to John. Every time he called he was reassured that everything was on track.

John learned that the brokers did not have his best interest at hand. John decided to sue. Let me clarify when I say "sue". Anyone who has an account at a major brokerage firm or bank agreed to never sue them. You are not allowed. When the new account paperwork is signed there is a little box that you are asked to check off. The box that you so innocently checked off states that you agree to never sue. This is the same agreement you sign when you purchase a car. If you have a problem with your car, you cannot sue – you must go through arbitration. If you don't check off this box, they will not open your account. Consequently if you have a bad investment , lose a large sum of money or feel you have been misled… you cannot take them to court. You are required to go through an arbitration panel. An arbitration panel will rotate though a geographical area hearing complaints from various investors. So let's say Mr. Client has a problem with a brokerage firm. Mr. Client will normally wait two to three months for the arbitration proceeding to begin. The arbitration panel will consists of 3 - 5 individuals. The panel will "hear" your complaint.

Getting back to our story, John found out that he was not allowed to sue, so he went to arbitration. As typical in these cases a victory was awarded to John. He was awarded $10,000. That is not a misprint, it is ten thousand dollars. The arbitrators essentially said "we are sorry you lost $1.1 million dollars but here's $10,000 now go away". You have no recourse, zero, because you can't go to civil court and you can't go to criminal court. The arbitrator's decision is binding. If you do not agree to go to arbitration (checking the box on the application) they are not going to open that account for you. Major investment firms are not going to open their checkbook to potential lawsuits from disgruntled clients, hence the arbitration process.

The gentleman in the article did however learn a valuable secret regarding money management. As the arbitration process unfolded, various things were pointed out to him. He was shocked to learn that his financial advisors had no legal obligation to act in his best interest.

You read that correctly. While a broker is required to offer suitable investments they are perfectly within their legal rights to ignore the investments that are best for you. If their options are to put your money into a high commission, underperforming investment that pays them a big fat commission and high fees compared to offering you a more appropriate investment that pays them a lower fee, there is nothing prohibiting them from putting you in that lemon that is best for them and not so good for you.

Unfortunately, they are within their legal right to put your money in the investment that makes them the most money, regardless if it is in your best interest or not. The article goes on to state, "the rules that differentiate a broker from a registered investment advisor (again a broker has the Series 6, Series 7 or Series 63 and registered investment advisors have the series 65) predate World War II. "Unlike a broker, a registered investment advisor is considered a true fiduciary which means they are legally required to act in your best interest at all times." While a broker is required to offer you a suitable investment they are perfectly within their legal right to ignore the investment that would be best for you. That pretty well sums it up, and answers the question as to why there is so much bad investment advice being provided. If it comes down to earning a commission or not — will they ignore the value of morality and integrity or will they do what is best for you?

So it would seem when you are shopping for an investment advisor all you have to do is ask to see their investment license. If they have the Series 65, you should be in good shape, your best interest will be served. Right? Well not always. Commissioned based advisors have recently added the Series 65 to their arsenal of licenses. In many cases if they state they have a Series 65, they may also have a Series 6, 7 or 63 which allows them to offer investments that pay an up-front commission paid out of your money. The only way to be sure is to make sure the Series 65 is the only license they have. Because if the Series 65 is the only license they have they are prohibited from selling investment that pay them a commission.

Check your statement. If you have commission mutual funds or variable annuities then you can be certain you are paying high commission and fees that normally never appear on your statement. Did they forget to put those fees and commissions on your statement? Of course not, read the fine print on your statement where it says "please refer to your prospectus for additional information". The additional information is the fee structure that is buried in the 200 page plus prospectus that no one ever reads. If you do have some of those investments call your advisor and ask. Ask why they were never disclosed. It is your money, you have a right to know.

The preceding information alone can save you literally tens of thousands of dollars. Bottom line: you need to ask questions, lots of questions. You need to understand your investments and how your advisor works. Are they working for you or are they working for their firm and their commission?

Retirement Accounts

Next I want to discuss retirement accounts. When I say retirement accounts, it's anything that hasn't been taxed yet. It can be an IRA, 401K, 403B, 457 deferred comp, PERS, etc., anything that hasn't been taxed. If the money has not been taxed it is referred to as "qualified money". The one thing that all retirement accounts have in common is they have not been taxed. This section refers to making sure your retirement accounts are set up correctly to ensure if something happens to you the IRS doesn't become one of the biggest beneficiary of your estate. Money Magazine recently had an article entitled <u>From Debtors to Millionaires</u>. The article references a 66 year old man who died suddenly and his 37 year old son was his primary beneficiary. The man who passed away was preceded in death by his wife.

Consequently, his son was next in line with respect to being the beneficiary. The deceased gentleman had been able to save over $500,000 in his 401K. Saving over a half a million dollars is a noble accomplishment and a result of dedicated saving and budgeting for many years. The last thing anyone wants to happen is to have their hard earned life savings be diverted away from their family. No one wants the IRS to be one of the largest beneficiaries to their estate. Leave your assets to your family, not the government.

The father in the article was a meter reader for about 38 years. It took him much of his life to save his $500,000 retirement account. When the father died unexpectedly the son received a call informing him that he was the sole beneficiary to his father's 401K. Since the father's wife had preceded him in death, his account was left directly to his son. The son was certainly surprised to learn his father had saved over a half million dollars. He had no idea his father had saved that much money.

Unfortunately, it wasn't quite the windfall that it initially seemed. The father hadn't received the best advice when he opened this account with respect to beneficiary designations. The article states, "Unfortunately his father's 401K was not quite the windfall it seemed."

As a non-spousal beneficiary, the son must take the money as a lump sum which will generate an estimated $230,000 tax bill. Since the account was not set-up properly, the IRS ends up being one of the biggest beneficiaries of the estate.

Let's walk through this and see what should have been done differently to protect the money for his family. The illustration I am going to use is $500,000. I use this amount only because that is what is referenced in the article. This amount can certainly be much greater or a lot less, but the structuring of the account would be the same. The father had $500,000. At his death $230,000 was taken out as tax.

So the son was left with $270,000, the IRS received $230,000 for doing nothing.

Let's look at this example analytically: $500,000 account, $230,000 was taxed which left the son $270,000. The account should have been structured as follows: The son being 37 could have taken control of his father's IRA at his father's death.

However, to accomplish this the 401K would have to be rolled over to an IRA prior to the father's death. Since the money was qualified, the son would have had to take what's called an RMD which stands for required minimum distribution. Anyone who is over 70 ½ is required to take the RMD every year after their 70 ½ birthday. The RMD amount starts out at about 3.7% of the account value. For example, if the IRA account has a value of $100,000, $3700 would be required to be taken from the account in the first year of RMD distribution. Every year as you age you are required to take out a little bit more. The mandatory withdrawal amount established by the IRS increases every year. The IRS wants to make certain they collect all of their tax money before the account holder walks through the pearly gates or south of the pearly gates.

Getting back to our example, the IRS wants their money somehow - some way. If the son takes ownership of his father's IRA (which he can do if set-up correctly prior to the IRA's original owner's death). The son could have had the option to elect ownership of his dad's IRA. Since it was inherited the son would have had to pay an RMD, but the RMD amount would have been based on his son's age. The deceased father's IRA would be classified as a Beneficiary IRA in the name of the beneficiary. The RMD payment would actually be based on the son's age.

For this example the RMD or LEP amount would only be approximately 2% or $10,000. So out of that $500,000 dollars the son would be required to withdraw only $10,000 and pay tax only on that $10,000.

Instead of paying tax on the entire $500,000 his tax liability would have only been on $10,000.

If that original $500,000 compounded at 5% by the time the son got to be retirement age the original amount would have been worth approximately $3 million dollars with reinvestment of all dividends and earnings. Let's take this a step further. In this specific example there are also two grandchildren involved here; a two year old and a four year old. The son could have said he was going to keep $300,000 and given $100,000 to each of his two children (ownership under a custodial account).

The parent keeps control of the money. This action is allowed by the IRS and it is called Disclaiming. The law was passed in 2001 and referred to as a Multigenerational or Stretch IRA.

Many people don't even know this law exists and a lot of brokerage firms and banks don't teach their investment advisors about it because it doesn't make them any money. The multigenerational or stretch IRA lets the beneficiary stretch the inherited IRA out for as many generations as they possibly can. So if the $500,000 account was set up the correct way initially, by the time those two grandchildren were of retirement age the account would have been worth approximately $8 million dollars compounded at just 6% interest annually.

The grandfather would have been able to create a legacy for his family instead of having the IRS take nearly half of his life savings. Money that was intended for his family.

Structuring the IRA properly puts the power and the control into the hands of the beneficiary, not the IRS. If the beneficiary wants to take the money out as a lump sum, then fine, they can take the money out but they will have to claim it as ordinary income and pay tax on the amount. The account can also be established so the beneficiary has the control. The account can remain tax deferred and continue to grow with no large tax implication. As Albert Einstein said, "the greatest discovery in his lifetime was compound interest."

Moral of the story: set your retirement accounts up so your beneficiaries win, not the IRS.

When you look at a multigenerational or stretch IRA there are three things you have to look at. Number one: the beneficiary document. Many custodians won't even administer this because it does not make them any money. You need to verify in writing that your custodian does indeed administer this type of account. You can't simply ask, you must see it in writing.

Secondly most advisors don't know they don't know. They have never been told about it, they have never been trained on the aspects of multi-generational IRA's.

Very importantly, make sure your beneficiary document is set up correctly. Many people can't put their hands on their beneficiary form, but you need to make sure it is updated to ensure it will keep your assets from going into probate.

Countless people think that if they have a will or a trust then everything is great. If the point comes when a court is involved a beneficiary form will trump a trust, and it will trump a will.

The Supreme Court has rules on such a case and the precedent is now set. The case is U.S. Supreme Court Ruling on Plan Beneficiary, Kennedy v Plan Administrator. The United States Supreme Court unanimously rules that an ex-spouse receives the retirement plan money, because she was named on the beneficiary form — even though she waived her rights to that money is a divorce decree. The beneficiary form trumps all.

Following are some basic facts of the case: the account holder died three years after he retired. His ex-wife was the beneficiary of his company plan balance of $402,000. He had worked 34 years for the company where he contributed to the company plan (a Savings and Investment Plan — an ERISA qualified plan).

He and his ex-wife divorced nine years prior to his death. Under the divorce decree, the ex-wife waived her rights to any benefits under his retirement plan. He wanted his plan balance of $402,000 to go to his daughter, but he never changed the beneficiary form on his plan. It still named his ex-wife — and the company paid plan paid the plan money to her as the named beneficiary even though she waiver her rights to that money in the divorce.

Beneficiary forms trump all other documents. This is a Supreme Court ruling which makes it the law of the land. This affects everyone. Companies will have this ruling behind them now to pay only the beneficiary named on the beneficiary form, regardless of what a will, a trust, a divorce decree, or other signed documents might say.

Make certain that what is on the will or trust matches up to what is on the beneficiary document. I bring this up because the beneficiary form becomes an afterthought for many people. They update their will and their trust, but they many times forget to update the beneficiary document.

A very important component of protecting retirement assets pertains to money in a 401k, 403B, 457 etc. If you have any money in a retirement account from a previous employer it is in your best interest to move it to a self-directed IRA. This is based on the premise of the flexibility you have in an IRA. You do not have that with an employer sponsored plan. You cannot set-up a multi-generational IRA in an employee sponsored retirement plan. If you have retirement funds at a former employer it is in your best interest to rollover those assets to an IRA. Make certain it is done correctly to ensure you do not incur negative tax consequences. Additionally, if you are 59 ½ and your current employer offers an in-service distribution you may be better served to move that money to a self directed IRA. If your current employer offers any type of matching, it makes the most sense to transfer 90% to an IRA and leave the remainder at your current employer to take advantage of the matching funds.

Now for my required disclaimer, since I am not an accountant please do not construe any of the aforementioned or following information as tax or legal advice. Please consult a qualified tax and/or legal professional

DO NOT LEAVE $ IN 401K.

CAN NOT TAKE ADVANTAGE OF IRS LAW.

ROLLOVER TO IRA FOR FULL ADVANTAGE!

If you leave your retirement funds in a 401K (403B, 457 Def Comp etc.) you are gambling with what is known as a non-spousal IRA. For example, if Joe has $300,000 in a 401K and his wife is his primary beneficiary and his children are his contingent beneficiaries. If Joe's wife pre-deceases Joe, the retirement money then goes to his children. Unfortunately, the children will have to claim the retirement proceeds from their father as ordinary income. They do not have the option to defer that money if it is in an employer sponsored account. If it is in a self-directed IRA then they can.

If you have an old 401K movie it into a self-directed IRA because you can save your beneficiaries thousands and thousands of dollars in both real assets and potential tax liability.

Buy and Hold is an Outdated Model

The S&P 500 and the Dow lost big in 1987, 2001, 2002, 2008, and chances are quite high it will lose big again. Do they really care what happens to the market as long as you are fully invested at all times? As long as you are buying something, they are making money.

According to Wealthbuilder.com private investors lost a cumulative total of $6 – $8 trillion in 2008 – 2009 due to the stock market meltdown. Dow Lones calculated the monetary value lost in the stock market from October 9, 2007 through March 5, 2009 was greater than 50%. Using simple math, if someone had $300,000 invested in the Dow Jones on October 9, 2007, five months later they only had $150,000 left. So they lost 50% of their money. I hear many people say, "but I don't buy stocks, I buy mutual funds."

Where do you think most mutual funds invest their money? They invest it in stocks. According to SmartMoney, the average mutual fund loss in domestic equities for 2008 was 37.6% and a loss of 45.8% for international equities. The facts tell the story as to why the average investor in mutual funds and variable annuities saw such huge losses to their life savings.

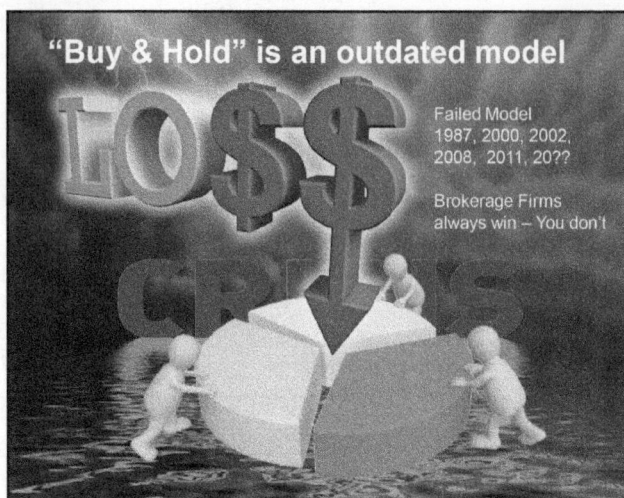

"Buy & Hold" is an outdated model

Failed Model
1987, 2000, 2002,
2008, 2011, 20??

Brokerage Firms
always win – You don't

Stocks lost 30% in 1987, 45% in 2001 & 2002, lost 39% in 2008 and will lose big again. It's only a matter of time.

The buy and hold model has been proven to be an abject failure. It is outdated and history proves the point. The reason the buy and hold model is still trumpeted as an effective model is because it makes the brokerage firms, banks and mutual fund companies money. There is nothing wrong with making money, just as long as everyone is on the same page.

During the time period of the 1980s through the 1990s, the Wall Street brokers were telling the investing public that the best strategy to make money was to "buy and hold". They said it did not make sense to try and time the market, but a better course of action was to just buy the investment, forget about it and hold onto it for the long term. Buy and hold only works in a long term bull market, when the market is steadily increasing. Those long term bull markets are far and few between.

Most investors end up losing big. Some regain a portion of their losses back. Many do not. And the fortunate few who have regained their losses resulted in years of zero growth. They majority of investor do not have the patience or time on their side to sit idly by for 5–6 years just hoping and waiting to get back the money they lost. Not a great way to grow and secure your money.

Not all investors lose big when the markets correct. There are some investors who experience significant gains because their investments were properly positioned.

It is not a matter of if the stock market will correct again; it is a question of when. History provides up with some strong clues concerning the volatility of the stock market. The stock market goes up and the stock market goes down. This is not some new revelation. We all know this (or at least we should). The significant element is to be positioned correctly.

The majority of investors lose money because they don't realize how much risk they really have. Many investors do not understand the risk in their investments. It is not a function of intelligence or education – it is a function of awareness. For many the investment world is like trying to understand a hieroglyphics.

When they look at their statements they truly don't understand the risks, the liquidity, the fees or the general intent of the investment. When people open their statement and see they have lost 10%, 20% 30% or more, the first thing they say is, "What happened, where did my money go?" In a panic, they call their financial advisor and are told "don't worry, it's just a paper loss" or "we are in this for the long term". What a load of you know what, it is NOT a paper loss, it is real money, and it was your money and now it's gone.

Many people have so much more risk in their investments than they realize. The risk factor becomes exceedingly more important the older someone becomes. Especially if they are retired or nearing retirement.

If you lose a chunk of money, how do you get it back? You don't go back and work for another 30 to 40 years. Losing money isn't exactly how people expect to spend their retirement years, but that's what happens to most people's investments. Just like a roller coaster; they ride it all the way up, then they ride it all the way down and wait for it to come back and then they do same thing all over again.

Unfortunately, the previous scenario is how the average investor's portfolio performs. Just like a roller coaster up and down, up and down, up and down. When it comes to investing the "buy and hold" model is based upon a failed premise. Following is some factual information to corroborate the preceding statement.

Here's the real story. The brokerage industry tells everybody to stay in the stock market for the long term and you can earn 8% or more. Well, that's only part of the story. Those 7% – 8% earning periods come in big chunks of 30–35 years. In addition to that, there are long time frames where there's zero growth. That's right, zero, nothing, zilch.

The historic numbers equate to 74 years of 0% growth and only 38 years of 7%. That's roughly a 67% chance to make 0% or a 33% chance to make 7%. The odds are nearly 2:1 that you lose. And that is exactly why the majority of investors earn little or nothing on their investments.

You have heard the term bull market and bear market. If you add the complete cycle you have an approximate 25–30 year cycle before everything goes full circle. I'm not trying to predict the future, no one can. Nevertheless, in the investment world history does repeat itself.

Historic cycles are based on stock valuations, price earnings ratio, various market metrics and a variety of other factors which ultimately relate to how much a stock is worth. When you look at the stock market historically there are definitely bullish (good times) and bearish (bad times). For most investors it is the luck of the draw of when they get in and when they get out and most importantly what type of investments are utilized while they are "in" the market. Luck is no way to plan for a secure future.

If you go back to 2000 until 2013 and you take the very best 100 days of the stock market you would have had a +376% return. That's great. If you were fully invested then in the worst 100 days you lost 377%. So your net return was

.6%, just a hair over ½% for 12 years of risking your hard earned money.

Simple question: "does it make sense to be invested 365 days a year?"

The answer is "it depends". I know that is not a very definitive answers. If someone uses a typical buy and hold model then the answer is no. If they are positioned when their investments can profit in a down market, the answer is perhaps. And if the market is really in disorder and can't decide which way is up or down the investments are best protected by moving them to cask (money market or short-term T-Bills).

Your investments must be able to withstand all types of market conditions both good and bad. Most people have a "hope and a prayer" portfolio. They hope it does good and they pray it does not do bad. Don't get me wrong, I'm all for prayer and I do it on a very daily basis. I just don't know how closely God watches the stock market.

Risk and reward need to be balanced. The real truth is that an investor does not have to take undue risk for a substantial reward. Risky investments do not equate with exceptional returns. Risky investments simply equate to losing money.

As mentioned, the average investor took all the risk but they didn't make most of the money. The brokerage firm takes no risk, but they are always making money.

How and Ice Cream Stand is Similar to the Stock Market

Without getting into a long drawn out dissertation on financial analysis, the PE, (price earnings) tells a big part of the story. To explain PE I will use a brief example of the local ice cream store down the street from where you live. Let's say that that ice cream stand on the corner makes $100,000 per year selling ice cream cones.

Let's also say the person who owns that ice cream stand wants to sell it and they want to sell it for $2 million dollars. That ice cream stand would have a PE ratio of 20. That means that they want to sell it for 20 times more than it's actually earning. So if you have an ice cream stand that is making $100,000 a year and somebody wants to sell for $ 2 million dollars it means the ice cream stand would be selling for 20 times earnings. $2,000,000 (asking price) is 20 times more than the annual earnings of $100,000.00, resulting in a PE of 20. Knowing what you now know about the ice cream stand, do you think that it would be a good investment? Would you invest $2,000,000 to make $100,000 per year? Would you buy it? Hopefully, you answered no. You would have to keep that ice cream stand for 20 years and hope it continued to make $100,000 per year, just to get your original investment back. I think you would agree, this would not be the best investment.

The ice cream stand example is basically similar to how the stock market works. Granted there are more moving parts of the stock market, in its essence PE tells the story. All stocks have a price earnings ratio. According to history when the price earnings ratio approaches 21, 22, 23 and beyond they are nearing an overvalued position with not much upside potential. In plain English, there is a much greater chance for that stock to lose value than there is for it to increase in value. Historically anytime the market experienced a major correction; 1929, 1966, 1987, 2001, 2002, 2008, the PE ratios were inflated and overvalued. Stocks get so over valued there's limited upside potential. The sell-off starts, and over a period of a few weeks or months the stock will lose a considerable portion of the value. This results with the investor losing a large sum of money.

The stock market did well when the Pes were low in 1921, 1954, and 2000. Stock Market did not do well when the Pes were high in 1929, 1966, 2008, 2012.

It is exceedingly difficult to time the market. Next to impossible. However trends can be identified and capitalized upon. Trend following can be used very effectively and successfully.

Unfortunately, many still think the stock market today is the same as it was in the 70s, 80s, and 90s. To put in into perspective the long-term bull market is a thing of the past. The past bull market fueled primarily by the baby boomer generation. They were buying houses, cars, appliances, and items for their children. They were also fully employed in strong and stable manufacturing career. Careers that supported the manufacturing boom of that era. The market was fueled by a very strong and large demographic sector known as the baby boomers. Those same baby boomers are now retiring or planning for retirement. 10,000 baby boomers are turning 65 years old every day. They are not supporting the economy as they once did.

If buy and hold had proven to be an abject failure then why is it still recommended by Wall Street? The answer is that the buy and hold strategy is self-serving to the companies that recommend it.

It is rare that it makes sense to be fully invested at all times. There are definite time periods when it makes more sense to be in cash or investments that can profit in a downward trending market.

The average investor must ask themselves a basic question, "How much risk do I want in my investment portfolio?" The answer is usually "not much". However, when their portfolio is reviewed in detail it becomes apparent that their portfolios contained significantly more risk than they had signed up for.

There are different types of risk. There is interest rate risk, equity risk and liquidity risk just to name a few. More times than not, the client was not aware of risk their investments were exposed to.

Losing value is only part of the problem. The time required to make up those losses can be the real issue.

Especially when someone is near or in retirement the time it takes to potentially regain what you lost can be a very long drawn out ordeal. When you lose a large portion of your assets, how do you get it back? Do you go out and work for another 20 years? Probably not, time is not on your side.

If you lost just 10% and you earn a consistent 3% return with NEVER a down year, it will take 3.6 years to get your money back. When you lose 20% it takes 7.5 years.

That isn't where you want to be. You don't always want to be waiting on getting your money back. You want to move forward not backwards. Two steps forward and no steps backwards is much better than one step forward and two steps back. If you play catch-up it is very difficult to move forward.

When you lose money in the stock market, how long does it take to get it back?		
If your portfolio is down:	Rate of Return	
	3%	6%
	Years to rebuild your portfolio	
10%	3.6	1.8
20%	7.5	3.8
30%	12.1	6.1
40%	17.3	8.8
50%	23.4	11.9

Why Do You Own the Investments You Do?

Why do you own the investments that you own? Let's think about this, if the investment firms you are dealing with have the best research and the smartest individuals then you should have the best investments, right? You would think that all the big firms have the best analysis, consequently you should have the best investments. The answer is not always yes and many times the answer is no.

There are approximately 10,000 mutual funds to choose from. Why do you own the ones that you own? If you picked them yourself that's fine, but if they were recommended to you, then why were they recommended? There was a recent article in The Wall Street Journal titled <u>Why a Broker Giant Pushes Mediocre Mutual Funds</u>. A line from the article states, "Like many who bought poorly performing mutual funds and variable annuities, Nancy lost big. What this 70 year olds' broker never told her was that he had a strong incentive to sell specific mutual funds over another." The nationally known brokerage firm receives hefty payments up to $100 million dollars a year to recommend certain funds over others.

When training its brokers most brokerage firms only tell their brokers about the funds that pay them the highest fees and never mention the other investments. "The deception is that the broker seems to give objective advice", says Taymar Frankle, a law professor of Boston University who specializes in mutual fund litigation. In fact, he says "the brokers are paid more for pushing only certain funds."

Within the brokerage industry investments are often sold as part of a sales contest.

The contest winners can win golf clubs, golf bags, fishing trips, vacations, you name it. I saw first-hand; investments being sold for the sole purpose of winning a very nice golf bag, a golf driver, even a very exclusive deep see fishing trip to Bermuda, trips to San Diego, you name it I saw it. All expenses paid for the winners and the guest. Many advisors didn't care if the investment was good or not, the only thing many of them cared about was if they were going to Bermuda.

Two major brokerage firms were fined $19.4 million dollars for improper sales contests. In another contest, another major brokerage firm failed to adequately disclose revenue sharing payments that it received from a select group of mutual fund companies to offer their funds over others. You have to be careful and understand why you have the investments you do.

You need to remember the brokerage firms and banks have a certain business model their employees must follow. They are required to sell only certain types of investments. And most often those investments have the highest fees and the most risk. "Why?" To make money for the company, not the investor.

We are living in very different times with respect to investments. The investment world today is nothing like it was even 10 years ago. Some of the best investments previously available have been put on the shelf by the brokerage firms and banks. They have been forgotten about and not utilized. Why have such fine investments been relegated to the closet? Why have some of the good investments been kept away from the average investor? The answer is simple. Money.

The brokerage firms have always operated on the commission based model just as they do today. However, there is one stark difference. In the "good old days" (I sound like my father) an investment advisor could offer their clients good investments and make a decent living. A reasonable commission was paid to an advisor when they positioned their clients in the proper investments. The client did well, the advisor did well, and the brokerage firm did well. However, in the endless searching for increased shareholder value and higher profits the investment industry firms had to figure out a way to make more money. Bring more dollars to the bottom line. So how were they going to do that?

It wasn't too long before the brokerage firms figured out they (the investment firm) could make considerably more money by "selling" their clients investments that made the investment firm more money. How would the investment firm make more money? By extracting more fees out of the client's money and putting it in the pockets of the investment firm and a portion of it to their advisors. The more the advisor would sell the higher the payout they would receive. Do you see any conflict of interest with this model?

There was only one catch. If the investments were costlier for the client and if the client knew of all the costs, commissions and risk, would they still decide to invest their money? Probably not. The answer to this dilemma was actually pretty simple. The investment firms figured if they reduced the commissions that were paid to advisors for the good quality investments and increased their commissions to the advisors when they sold the investments that made the firm more money then it would only be a matter of time before the investments that generated the most revenue for the firm would be recommended most often.

And that is exactly what has happened. Investment firms and commissioned investment advisors make the most money when they "sell" you the costlier investments.

Here are just a few examples of some of the more common investments and their commissions paid to the advisor who "sold" the investment.

▶ REIT (Real Estate Investment Trust): 7-9% average commission paid to the advisor from your money.

▶ Limited Partnership: 7-8% average commission paid to the advisor from your money.

▶ Variable Annuity: 7% average commission paid to the advisor from your money + 3-4% annual fees

▶ Mutual Fund A: 5.75% average commission paid to the advisor from your money + annual fees

▶ Mutual Fund C: 6% average commission paid to the advisor form your money + annual fees

With an average commission of 6.75% (NOT including latent fees) for every $100,000 you invest $6,750 is being deducted from your account BEFORE the investment is ever made. So you need to earn $6,750 just to break even and get your own money back before you can even think about turning a positive return on your investment. Factoring in other fees, market losses, and commissions it's not hard to figure out why your investment accounts have a difficult time making money.

The best way to protect yourself is to first make certain you NEVER purchase an investment where the advisor is paid an up-front commission from your money. This is step #1 to protect yourself. To make it simple, just ask your advisor how they get paid, how much and where does the money that pays them come from.

Over the years, the costlier investments have overtaken the investment world. It is for this reason the majority of investors have a portfolio full of mutual funds, variable annuities, REITS and Limited Partnership. They generate the most money for the investment advisor and the investment firm in terms of commissions and fees. You need to remember the term "shareholder value". The goal of every major investment firm is to make money for their shareholders.

There is no such thing as the "perfect investment for everyone". Whenever I hear someone say they were told a specific investment is "perfect" then I suggest they put their hand over their wallet and run the other way. Before any investment can be recommended, a thorough analysis needs to take place to decipher what is "best" for the respective individual.

Brokerage firms and commissioned financial advisors will go to endless lengths to make Americans believe that mutual funds, variable annuities, REITS, etc. along with the old buy and hold model is a sure path to investment success.

Many financial advisors continually speak of a mythical mutual fund or variable annuity that will produce a fantastic return "over the long haul." This is in stark contrast to the data. Dalbar, one of the nation's largest investment research firms, found mutual funds have only yielded returns of 3.6% over a twenty year period. And that 3.6% return was before fees.

According to the WSJ stocks have averaged just a 5.5% annual gain on an inflation-adjusted basis since 1912. This rate of return may be a "historical freak" that isn't likely to be duplicated anytime soon due to slowing economic growth around the globe and the changing demographics of the United States.

Is it true that the good old days of the stock market are a thing of the past? Is the changing and aging demographic of the United States negatively affecting corporate growth and the stock market? Does computerized high frequency trading leave the average investor out? Will the proliferation of commissioned based investments continue to be pushed on the investing public?

If the answer is yes to one or all of the aforementioned questions, is there light at the end of the tunnel? Can the average investor still get a fair shake and really make money in the investment world? Is there a better method of investing where the typical investor is not at a disadvantage and can truly achieve consistent returns and downside protection of principal without all of the double talk, hidden agendas and sleight of hand?

The answer is "yes."

There is a Better Way

When Albert Einstein was asked, "what is the greatest discovery in your lifetime", he answered "compound interest". It is amazing what compound interest will produce in the way of earnings. Unfortunately, most investors use the formula of compound interest in reverse. They are constantly losing money and trying to recoup their losses.

There are numerous investment methodologies, convoluted algorithms, and a host of complicated ways to make money with your investments. Even though investing can be a complicated endeavor it most certainly can be kept easy to understand, straightforward, and transparent.

The Two Bucket Approach

The illustration on the next page show a strategy that can be utilized very effectively with the goal of generating excellent investment returns over a market cycle combined with liquidity.

1   **2**

Income Planning   **Moderately Conservative**

Our philosophy is simple: It's your money, it's your life, take control. Your investment portfolio should enable you to thrive in any market condition. This can be accomplished with proactive solutions. As in most everything: just because everyone else is doing it doesn't make it the best path to follow. The same is true with investing. Following the herd mentality is the surest path to mediocrity. We have stepped out of the herd and follow a path that gives the power to the client where they know the rules of the game and have the knowledge to choose what in their best interest.

Our investment model is based on two simple buckets. Bucket One is for income now or in the future. It can also be used for safe growth with no downside. Bucket One can be structured to provide a lifetime income stream that will never run out, even if you live to be 100 or longer. It can also provide 100% principal protection, upside potential with no downside risk. Participate when the market goes up but not lose if the market goes down. All gains are tax deferred even if it is outside of the qualified account (IRA etc.) Bucket One can create an income stream you cannot outlive, a paycheck for life. There is a 50% chance among married couples one will live to 92 and a 25% chance one will live to 97. Consequently, income planning is very important for most investors.

If you have plenty of income through pensions. Social Security, etc., and you don't need guaranteed income, that's great. If not, we can utilize Bucket One for income planning purposes. As mentioned, Bucket One can also be structured for safe accumulation with no risk of loss due to a bad market.

Bucket Two is for low-risk investments. Low risk does not man boring returns. Bucket Two is totally liquid. Your money is always available to you. There is no time frame commitment. Put your money in today and take it out tomorrow if you wish.

The goal of the two-bucket model provides for protection of principal, income, growth and liquidity. The amount allocated to each bucket it totally dependent on each individual and their specific requirements and objectives. Some clients have a large portion of their money in Bucket One, others have nothing. Many clients have their assets allocated between Buckets One and Two. Still, other clients have their assets equally allocated to each bucket and many variations in between. This is not a one size fits all solution. It is a customized plan regardless of what the investment goals may be. The key is to formulate the portfolio to satisfy the needs of the individual client ultimately providing the best solution.

Bucket One is used for current or future income, and safe accumulation and no risk to principal. Simple and straightforward. Bucket Two is comprised of non-correlated, risk-off, tactical investments. Wow, that sounds impressive. What does it mean?

Simple stated, depending on a client's individual needs, the assets invested in Bucket Two are spread between 10 and 15 (depending upon the amount of assets) investments. Every investment utilized does something entirely different from the others. This means your assets are very well diversified over a variety of varying asset classes. All of the varying asset classes are also different. This simply means they all invest in different ways.

No one knows what the future will bring. No one knows if the stock market will go up or down. No one knows if interest rates will go up or down and on and on. The two-bucket model affords the potential to profit in all markets both up and down while keeping income consistent and principal protected from major losses.

The tactical portion of the portfolio means that our investments can move to cash in the event the markets become very volatile. They move to cash (money markets or short-term T-Bills) and bonds that protect principal when things get crazy.

The risk-off portion is just that. When the markets turn volatile the managers will turn the "risk-off" and move to safe ground or to investments that can profit in down trend environments.

It is very important to note that when it is appropriate to make a change within a portfolio there is not a cost to implement any change. Since we are a fee based advisor we do not charge trading fees etc.

The type of investments utilized are not the type of commission-laden, hidden-fee, risky types of investments discussed earlier. With respect to the investments in Bucket Two, we have formulated partnerships with, in our opinion, some of the country's very best private wealth managers.

Our goal in forming partnerships with the respective private wealth managers is to facilitate how we can best serve our clients and how we can bring them the very best investments for their individual needs. Additionally, our private wealth manager partnerships are not static in nature. We are constantly looking to partners with the best of the best and are willing to increase our partnerships with the wealth managers that meet our stringent criteria.

Our target is to utilize some of the most effective and exceptional private wealth managers in the country. We know that many investors would never have access to these very special wealth managers. The wealth managers I am speaking of normally have minimum investments of $1,000,000. Therefore, to be able to design a high quality, diversified portfolio a minimum of $5,000,000 would be required.

The reality is that most people do not have $1,000,000 or $5,000,000 of investable assets. Does this mean that most investors are stuck with the retail type of investments that were referenced earlier? Of course not. Our objective is to provide access to some of the best wealth managers available and have their proficiency and knowledge obtainable to a wide range of investors with varying amounts of investable assets.

Regardless of the size of our client's portfolio, we treat all clients with the utmost respect and professionalism. The value of a person is not determined by the size of their investment portfolio.

Many investment firms will not deal with a client unless they have assets in excess of $500,000. I do not agree with this mentality. I strongly feel a person with a smaller portfolio should have access to the same expertise, client care and professional money management as someone with a larger portfolio.

When I mention we deal with exclusive private wealth managers, the term "exclusive" can be an arbitrary word. To put their elite status in perspective you must realize there are hundreds of private wealth managers in the United States. We established a very stringent set of criteria that would enable us to identify only the best of the best wealth managers nationwide. When our strict criteria is applied, only a small fraction of the private wealth managers available can meet the rigorous criteria.

There are essentially three ways to invest. The first way is the "do it yourself" approach. This approach usually results with investment gains in the range of nothing to not very good, combined with the potential for a significant loss of principal. The method is also combined with a good dose of frustration and many sleepless nights.

The second way is the manner in which most people invest. It is called, retail investing. This is when the investors are sold investment products just like they are sold items from a retail store. Everyone knows that buying retail is the most expensive way to purchase anything. The same thing goes for investments. Purchasing retail investments such as commissioned mutual funds, variable annuities, REITs, limited partnerships, etc., costs the most money and will also seriously risk your financial security. With this method you not only pay the most, your assets are also subjected to increased risk, volatility, and potential loss.

There is also a third way and in my opinion by far the best way to invest. This third method is the method that we utilize for our clients. This is a methos where an investor can access elite private wealth managers combined with complete transparency, real-time results, accountability and liquidity.

With this method there are no conflicts of interest, no commissions paid from your money, and no fees buried in fine print. Just pure performance. With this model everyone "has a vested interest in your investing success." Our success and the wealth managers' success is based entirely on your investment's success.

Logically speaking, if someone "sells" you a commission based investment with a 7% up front commission and that commission comes out of your money before your money is ever invested, where is the commissions based advisor's incentive to perform? There is no incentive to perform because the bulk of their compensation has already been paid. The only incentive they have is to get you to "buy". After you have been sold the investment, their job is done. They have already been paid, from your money. If your investment does bad "oh well, sorry" what recourse do you have. You call your advisor and inquire about the loss, the normal reply is "it will come back" or "stay the course we are in this for the long term". What else can they say? Do they really care how your investments perform if the vast majority of their compensation has already been received?

When you compare the commission based model to the fee based performance model, there is a stark difference between the two. By comparison, with the fee based model, your investment accounts need to be kept productive and earning good rates of return for many years.

When you are sold a commission based investment and the advisor is paid a hefty commission directly from your money before the investment was ever made their job is essentially done. You were sold a product and they got paid. Just like the used car example.

Fast forward a year or two. If your investment is not performing very well and you decide to search for better investing alternatives and part ways with your current advisor they may be upset because they will lose their "trail" commission. However the vast majority of their compensation was received the day you wrote the check. You paid them before you knew how your investment was going to perform.

Conversely, with the fee based model such as we use, if you are not happy you are free to leave with no strings attached. The stark difference is that with the fee based model no one was paid up front. Since we are a fee based advisor we must earn your business quarter after quarter, year after year. To put it into perspective, we need to keep your as a happy productive client for nearly seven years to earn what a commission based advisor earns in one day. Yes that is correct, this is not a typographical error. Seven years vs. one day.

Where do you think your best interests are served? Is it with someone who gets paid day one, when you are sold a product? Or are your best interests served by someone that is paid over the long term based on excellent performance and customer service for many years. We do not sell products. We offer wealth management solutions designed to grow and protect your wealth. We also build sustainable client relationships that continue to strengthen and grow year after year.

Investing is for building financial security through your working years leading to financial security through retirement. Retirement is something that happens to most everyone. Retirement today is vastly different than it was years before.

When someone retires today their money needs to last 20, 30, 40 years. They MUST protect what they have since it needs to last them a very long time. When you are 50 and younger you should be in the accumulation stage of investing. You need to be saving as much as possible to fund a secure retirement. Ages 50–65 investors need to protect their principal to make certain it does not go backward and lose value. They also need to maintain steady growth to counter inflation as well as providing for a comfortable life style.

Ages 65 and beyond can be defined as the years of preservation. Preservation encompasses a variety of elements including growth to keep pace with inflation, income to maintain one's lifestyle, liquidity to provide funds in times of need along with diversity and flexibility to be able to navigate whatever the investment landscape may throw our way. Number one priority is preservation of principal and not going backwards.

One must be certain to preserve their principal, because if they lose it—how will they get it back? Certainly they will not go back to work for another 40 years. At this stage you need to be certain your assets are providing you with the best returns along with the most safety.

Always Learning

Being an investment advisor has taught me a lot. It has taught me a good lot about money, investing and also about people—both the good side and the bad side. Without a doubt the good is much more prevalent than the bad. It has taught me that unfortunately, way too many people are middles about their investment, they don't really understand what investments they have and many times needlessly lose money.

Everyone with investments need to be adamant about understanding their investment. Where and how their money is actually invested is critically important. They don't need to understand all of the inner workings, the financial analysis and specific details of the investment. But they do need to know if any money has been deducted from their account to pay someone a commission, how much they are paying in fees, what is their real rate of return, is their money available to them if they need it, how have their investments performed in both good and bad markets just to name a few. Most importantly, is the investment suitable for their individual situation?

Can Your Investments
Pass the Stress Test?

There is only one way to make certain your investments are the best they can be for your individual situation and that is to have them reviewed and explained to you in a non-biased way.

We offer a complimentary portfolio review and analysis. It is more like a "stress test" for your investments. We will put your investments on the treadmill cranked all the way up and see how they will perform. Will they stand strong or will they fall off? How will they perform in tough markets? How have they performed in past tough times? Of course past performance is no guarantee of anything. However it does provide considerable insight and historical perspective of how the investments will perform in the next bad market. After all, it is not who makes money in a good market that is important—it is who makes money in a bad market that is imperative.

Our investment stress test will show you the real health of your investments including, commissions, fees, safety, liquidity, past performance, projected future performance and overall risk.

Very importantly, our free investment stress test is performed with independent and unbiased third-party data.

Our objective is not to meet with you and tell you all of your investments are bad. Our objective is to provide you with a thorough investment portfolio analysis based upon independent third party information.

If through the analysis we find that what you have is not the best and can be improved on we will share our ideas with you on how to improve your investment portfolio. If we find what you have is good, we will explain to you why it is a good fit. We make use of recognized independent third party data that analyzes and evaluates investments in a strictly independent and autonomous side-by-side comparison. The completed analysis results in a very easy to read and understandable description of the best manner to move forward with respect to your individual investment goal and objectives. We will spend the time to review your results with your and to answer any questions you may have.

If appropriate we will also provide you with a precisely detailed financial plan tailored specifically for your specific situation and unique requirements.

After reviewing the plan and after you have had all of your questions answered you decide if the plan is in your best interest. If you feel the presented plan is indeed in your best interest we simply continue our conversation and then discuss the best way to move forward.

It is a two way street of open communication. It is all about doing what is in your best interest.

At the very least you will gain a better understanding of what is going on inside your current investment portfolio and if it aligns with your true investment objectives and risk tolerance.

Rest assured there is no sales pitch, no pressure. Just valuable and useful information you can use to protect your money. Information that you can use to literally save tens or even hundreds of thousands of dollars.

We are a boutique investment firm, which allows us to remain very close to our clients. Our size enables us to work with all of our clients one-on-one and offers the us the ability to learn all aspects of their financial objectives. We are partnered with literally some of the very best wealth managers in the country and we have access to the very finest investments available, in our opinion and research.

We are also partnered with one of the country's largest independent FDIC regulated custodians. The sole purpose of utilizing our custodian is for safe-keeping and protection of all assets. No one ever has access to your funds except you.

Very importantly all accounts have complete transparency. By transparency I mean you have full access at all time. 24 hours a day, seven days a week. You can always see exactly what you have, real time values, transparency in all fees, investment allocations, year-to-date performance, historical performance, etc. Everything is updated dynamically in real-time.

You will find investments through us that you will not find through the majority of investment firms both small and large. We are very unique in how we structure our business and our investment portfolios. We do not offer products, we offer a complete money management system and a total solution focused on you and your goals. Very importantly, we also build long term relationships with our clients.

Final Words

There are many things in life more important than money. God, health, family and helping others, at least in my mind. Money is a medium or counter if you will that enables you to provide for your family, help others and provide you with some semblance of security in an otherwise crazy world.

Hopefully, this brief book has provided you with some useful and tangible information that will help you protect your family, your savings and your investments. If you feel a complimentary consultation is appropriate, it would be my pleasure to meet with you and discuss any investment related questions you may have. Chances are that if you have this book, you have my contact information. If so feel free to contact our office directly.

Thank You,

Dino J. LoPresti

Our Process

We specialize in a money management system that offers complete transparency, liquidity and excellent potential returns in all market environments.

Our idea of low risk, low volatility investing combined with an active money management system where assets can be moved to protect principal in volatile markets offers a very attractive alternative to the old fashioned "buy and hold" mentality where investors are forced to "take their lumps" and watch their portfolios go up and down like a see-saw.

Our clients value our credibility, knowledge and value system centered around our goal of providing low risk, low volatility money management. Low risk and low volatility does not mean boring returns. We believe in a Retirement Designed Money Management System that provides our clients with a portfolio planned to protect principal with the goal of achieving excellent returns over a market cycle. We have unique access to a platform of exceptional investment models unavailable to many smaller independent advisors as well as larger investment firms.

We commit ourselves to providing our clients with dedicated and personalized service to help them reach their investment goals. We want our clients to have a better financial future and realize financial success. Your success is our success.